Plesiosaur Peril

To my extraordinarily wise and lovely wife, Cheryl Hebert. You are magnificent. — D.L.

ACKNOWLEDGMENTS:
My profound thanks to Cheryl Hebert, Isaac Loxton, Jason Loxton and Andre Hebert for photographic assistance, useful insights and many other forms of help as well. Additional underwater photography was contributed for use in this book by Cheryl Hebert, Raj Pal, Remy Reijs, Scott Tucker, Sandy Gibson, Julie Roberts, Jeff Green and Daniel Abraham. A hat tip to many of my fellow writers and science advocates for supporting this series — including Marie-Claire Shanahan, Phil Plait and Andrew Mayne — and to the generations of paleoartists and paleontologists whose work inspired me to create it. Though she can never read this, I extend my thanks to sharp-eyed, hard-knuckled fossil-hunter Mary Anning (1799–1847) for introducing plesiosaurs to humanity. Nature looks deeper and richer for her discoveries.

Special thanks in particular to Darren Naish for his expert paleontological advice, and for giving so generously of his time and knowledge.

Additional thanks to my colleagues Pat Linse, Michael Shermer and William Bull at *Skeptic* magazine (www.skeptic.com) for their wisdom, support and ongoing encouragement.

Science consultation by Darren Naish.

Text and illustrations © 2014 Daniel Loxton

Kids Can Press acknowledges the financial support of the Government of Ontario, through the Ontario Media Development Corporation's Ontario Book Initiative; the Ontario Arts Council; the Canada Council for the Arts; and the Government of Canada, through the CBF, for our publishing activity.

Published in Canada by
Kids Can Press Ltd.
25 Dockside Drive
Toronto, ON M5A 0B5

Published in the U.S. by
Kids Can Press Ltd.
2250 Military Road
Tonawanda, NY 14150

www.kidscanpress.com

Edited by Valerie Wyatt
Designed by Julia Naimska

This book is smyth sewn casebound.
Manufactured in Tseung Kwan O, NT Hong Kong, China, in 10/2013
by Paramount Printing Co. Ltd.

CM 14 0 9 8 7 6 5 4 3 2 1

Library and Archives Canada Cataloguing in Publication

Loxton, Daniel, 1975–, author, illustrator
    Plesiosaur peril / written by Daniel Loxton ; illustrated by Daniel Loxton with Jim W.W. Smith.

(Tales of prehistoric life)
ISBN 978-1-55453-633-7 (bound)

    1. Plesiosauria — Juvenile literature. I. Smith, Jim W. W., illustrator II. Title. III. Series: Loxton, Daniel, 1975–. Tales of prehistoric life.

QE862.P4L69 2014   j567.9'37   C2013-903944-9

Kids Can Press is a **corus**™ Entertainment company

TALES OF PREHISTORIC LIFE

Plesiosaur Peril

Daniel Loxton

Illustrated by Daniel Loxton
with Jim W.W. Smith

Kids Can Press

The baby plesiosaur swam with her mother. Morning sunlight dappled their skin. Lazy waves rolled above their heads.

These plesiosaurs were *Cryptoclidus*, large creatures that traveled together in a family pod. Their flippers rose and fell like wings. They were flying underwater.

They soared over coral reefs. They swam between tropical islands.

Mother and baby rose gently to the surface. They breathed deeply. Salty air filled their lungs.

Plesiosaurs were reptiles, like their cousins the dinosaurs. They could not breathe underwater and had to come up for air.

Their babies did not hatch from eggs. They were born in the water, ready to swim. As they grew up, their mothers watched over them.

The plesiosaurs ruled their watery kingdom, but they were not alone. The oceans teemed with creatures. Some were large. Some were small. And some were enormous.

Jellies drifted with the tides. Fish flashed in silvery schools. Sharks prowled among them. Dolphin-shaped reptiles called ichthyosaurs dove deep. They hunted tentacled relatives of squids.

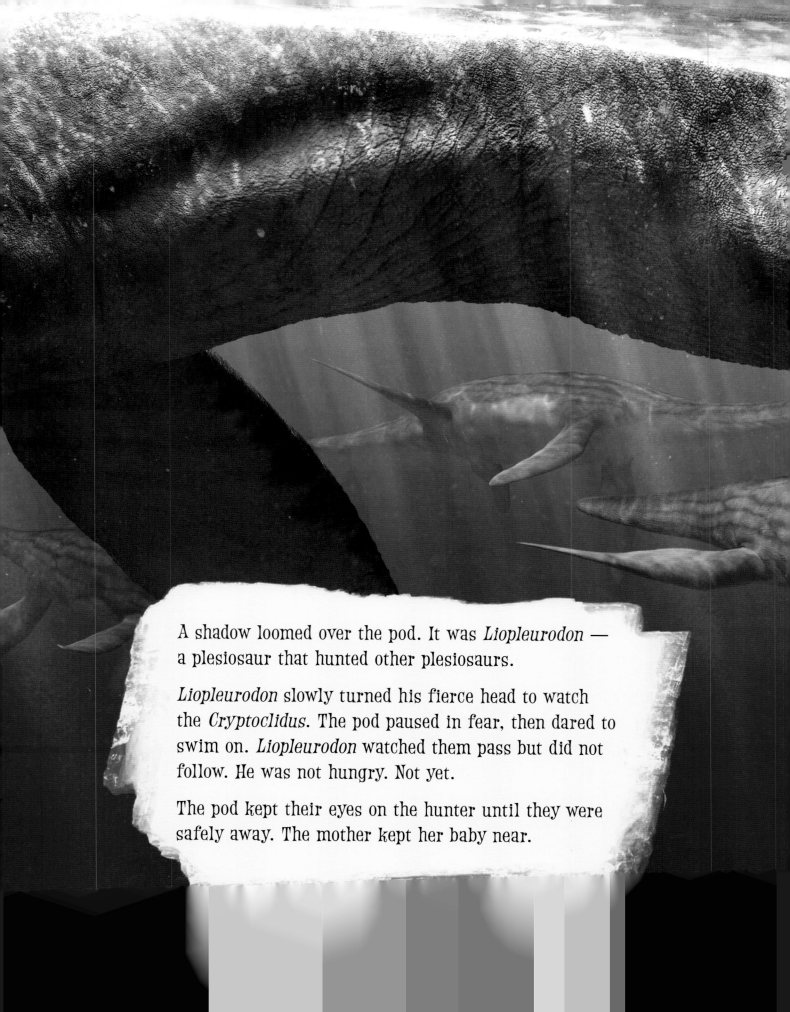

A shadow loomed over the pod. It was *Liopleurodon* —
a plesiosaur that hunted other plesiosaurs.

Liopleurodon slowly turned his fierce head to watch
the *Cryptoclidus*. The pod paused in fear, then dared to
swim on. *Liopleurodon* watched them pass but did not
follow. He was not hungry. Not yet.

The pod kept their eyes on the hunter until they were
safely away. The mother kept her baby near.

The wild ocean was dangerous but exciting. There was so much for the baby to explore. She followed her mother and learned by watching her.

She learned how to swallow stones to help digest her food. Not just any old stones would do. The pod traveled long distances to find just the right ones. The baby watched her mother choose smooth, round stones and swallow them one by one.

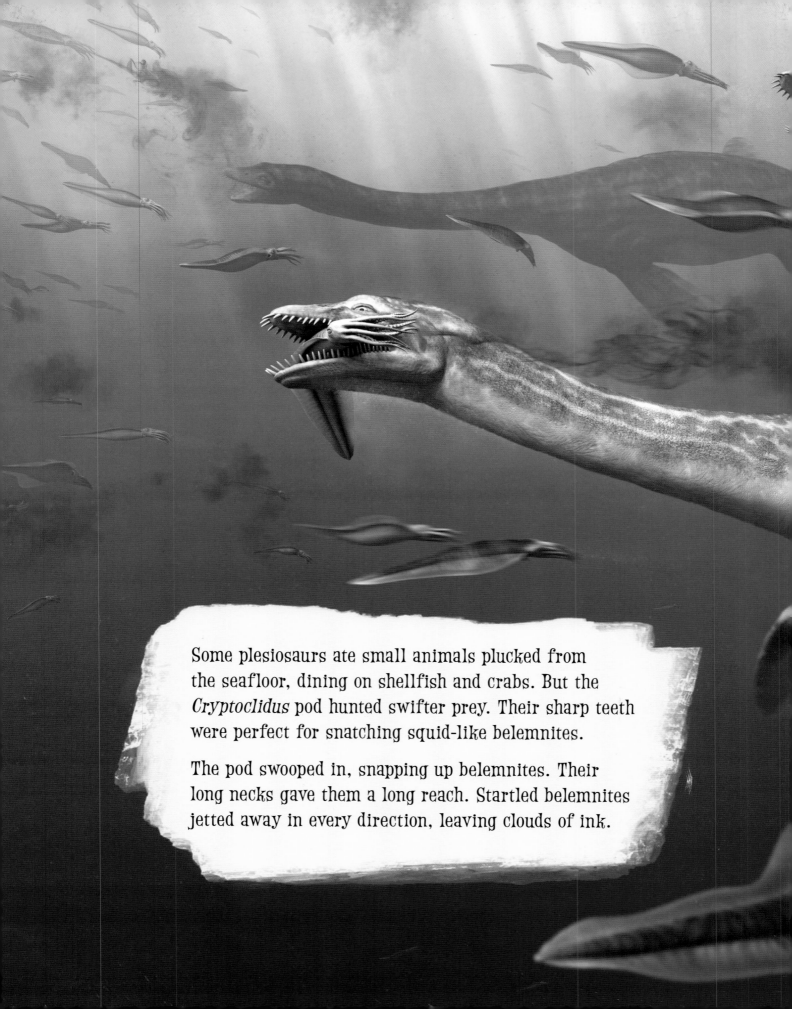

Some plesiosaurs ate small animals plucked from the seafloor, dining on shellfish and crabs. But the *Cryptoclidus* pod hunted swifter prey. Their sharp teeth were perfect for snatching squid-like belemnites.

The pod swooped in, snapping up belemnites. Their long necks gave them a long reach. Startled belemnites jetted away in every direction, leaving clouds of ink.

Everything was new to the baby *Cryptoclidus*. The
sea was full of sights and smells and tastes. As her
pod relaxed in the afternoon sun, she explored her
surroundings. She watched small fish dart over the
nearby reef. She nosed and nibbled among the colorful
sponges and corals. And then she spotted a tasty
belemnite.

She followed the tempting, tentacled snack. She
followed sparkles of sunlight.

The baby *Cryptoclidus* swam among a cluster of ammonites. The creatures hung almost motionless, as though suspended from sunbeams. Shifting patterns of light played over their shells. Their waving tentacles pulled in bits of food.

The little plesiosaur snapped and plucked playfully at their tentacles. She did not notice how far she had wandered. She was far from her mother. She was far from the safety of her pod.

What was that? A giant shadow slid slowly, slowly through the water. The baby *Cryptoclidus* turned toward it. Was it her mother?

No! The shadow was too big, and now it was moving faster. The baby watched nervously. Then the dark shape swam out of the gloom, and she jolted in terror. It was a hungry *Liopleurodon*!

The little *Cryptoclidus* spun around, trying to get away. But she was no match for *Liopleurodon*. His massive flippers propelled him toward her with shocking speed.

Cryptoclidus swam as fast as she could. Her flippers beat the water. She strained for escape with every muscle in her body.

Liopleurodon was a deadly hunter. He was big, he was strong — and he was gaining on his prey.

Suddenly, WHOOSH! The *Cryptoclidus* pod darted between hunter and hunted. Strength and speed are powerful forces in nature. But so is family. The pod swooped around the predator to distract him. The baby's mother whacked him with her flippers.

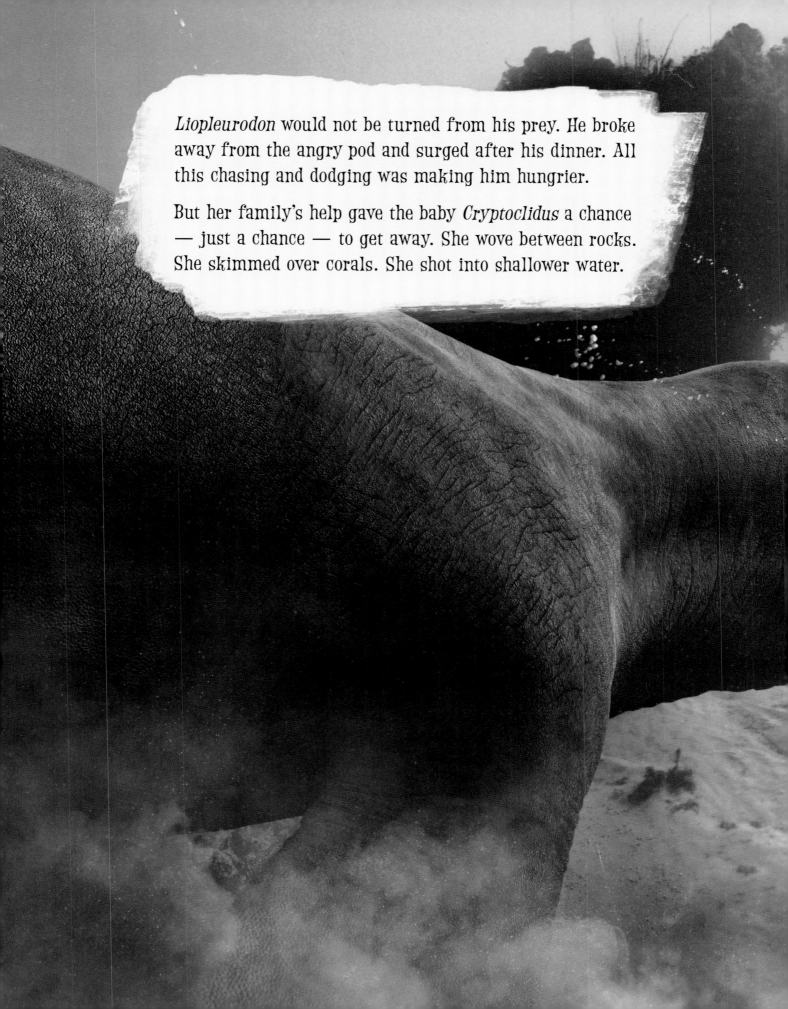

Liopleurodon would not be turned from his prey. He broke away from the angry pod and surged after his dinner. All this chasing and dodging was making him hungrier.

But her family's help gave the baby *Cryptoclidus* a chance — just a chance — to get away. She wove between rocks. She skimmed over corals. She shot into shallower water.

Liopleurodon followed, turn for turn. There! He had her cornered. His blood raced with excitement. His mouth ached with the urge to bite, bite, BITE!

The baby *Cryptoclidus* tried one last desperate move. She darted downward, then shot up toward the surface.

He reached for her, jaws open wide ...

But she was gone, cartwheeling up into the air and right over the reef.

KERSPLASH! The baby *Cryptoclidus* landed in the water on the other side of the reef. She looked back for *Liopleurodon*. The predator had turned away. He would find an easier meal. She was safe.

Soon her mother swam into sight, searching among the rocks and coral. The baby rushed to her side.

It was a big, wild, dangerous ocean, but they would swim it together. As a family.

Cryptoclidus and *Liopleurodon*

Cryptoclidus and *Liopleurodon* lived in the warm, shallow seas that covered Europe about 165 million years ago. *Cryptoclidus* was about as long as four grown men lying head to toe. *Liopleurodon* was about 3 m (10 ft.) longer and much stronger and heavier. Both were plesiosaurs — marine reptiles distantly related to dinosaurs. Plesiosaurs were the top ocean predators during the Jurassic period.

The events of this story are based on discoveries scientists made about the lives of these extinct animals. They found clues in fossils, the preserved remains of ancient creatures.

For example, they know that *Liopleurodon* were mighty hunters. Their huge cutting teeth left bite marks on the fossilized bones of plesiosaurs such as *Cryptoclidus*.

A recent fossil discovery suggests that plesiosaurs may have cared for their young, as the *Cryptoclidus* pod does in this story. Scientists found a fossilized plesiosaur with the bones of a baby inside. If the baby had grown enough to be born, it would have been far too big to be laid in an egg. This discovery tells us that plesiosaurs gave birth to live babies like whales and manatees do today.

Animal mothers who invest a lot of time and energy in one or two big babies often look after those babies. For example, whale mothers give birth to one large baby at a time and nurture the baby within the protection of a group — their pod. Plesiosaurs may have done so, too. Living in families is rare among reptiles but not unknown.